# The Seven Wonders
## of
# Washington State

Your guide to exploring the natural

wonders of the Evergreen State

Howard Frisk

Published by Howard Frisk Photography
P. O. Box 593
Sumner, WA 98390
www.HowardFriskPhotography.com

Printed by CreateSpace

ISBN-13: 978-1514112298
ISBN-10: 1514112299

Companion Web Site: SevenWondersofWashingtonState.com

Cover photo: the Palouse wheat fields in the spring as seen from Steptoe Butte
Back Cover photos: the Columbia River Gorge, Mt Rainier

*For my wonderful wife Penny, whose endless support is invaluable*

**Acknowledgements**

*I wish to thank the people who are a special inspiration for my photography: Brooke Shaden and Jessiann Loomis, and those who assisted me in the creation of this book: Sandra Lowen, Leah Williams and Ann Vargas*

# Contents

# Introduction

Come and explore the seven natural wonders of Washington State.

This book was created to highlight the seven natural wonders of Washington State. These seven locations are not part of any official list. They are based on my own travels and my own opinion on what are the most amazing places in this great state. I chose these locations because there is something very special about each one, they are easily accessible, and they provide opportunities to have personal experiences with the most fascinating places nature has to offer.

Several of the wonders of Washington State are one-of-a-kind geological formations that are found nowhere else in the world. Washington State is among the most ecologically diverse states in the country and each of the seven wonders represents a different aspect of that ecological diversity. Where else on Earth can you go from a rain forest to a desert in less than 100 miles?

Some of Washington State's natural wonders, such as Mt Rainier, are world famous. Every time I go to the Paradise Visitor Center I hear a multitude of languages being spoken by park visitors as I hike along the trails. People come here from all over the world to marvel at its massive glaciers, meadows bursting with millions of wildflowers, or autumn leaves exploding with color. On the other hand, some of Washington State's natural wonders, such as the Channeled Scablands, are virtually unknown, even to most of the residents of western Washington. The story of how the Channeled Scablands were formed is mind-boggling, and all the geological evidence is there for you to behold.

It is my hope that you will not be content to just peruse the photographs and read the superlative-laden comments, but more importantly, you will feel inspired to visit each one of Washington State's natural wonders and see them for yourself. This book is just a preview of the experiences that await you.

Mt Rainier as seen from the Sourdough Ridge Trail in the Sunrise area, with Little Tahoma Peak visible on the left

Mt Rainier is one of the most amazing places on earth. The original inhabitants of this area of our planet had various names for this mountain, one of them being Tahoma, which can be roughly translated as "God's home." We locals just call it "The Mountain". With 26 major glaciers, Mt Rainier is the most glaciated mountain in the contiguous US. At 14,411 feet, it rises higher above its surrounding mountains than any other mountain in the Cascade Mountain Range, making it one of the most massive mountains on Earth. Within the Mt Rainier National Park boundaries, you can find temperate rain forests, alpine meadows, rocky tundra, forested valleys, glaciers, hot springs, rivers, lakes, wildflowers in the summer and blazing fall foliage in the autumn. There is nothing else like it in the world, which is why it is the first wonder of Washington State.

Mt Rainier as seen from the Deadhorse Trail in the Paradise area

Mt Rainier is beautiful, but it is also an active and potentially dangerous stratovolcano. Although it has not erupted for about 1500 years, today there are dozens of steam vents, called fumaroles, under the ice at the summit. The fumaroles vent steam at 185 degrees, which continuously melt the ice at the summit. They have created the world's largest network of glacial caves, with almost two miles of passages and several small lakes (the highest in the world). At one time Mt Rainier was much higher than it is now. About 5,600 years ago the top 2,000 feet of the summit collapsed in a massive landslide which sent half of a cubic mile of mud and rocks (known as a lahar) racing down numerous valleys all the way to present day Tacoma and Seattle. A small lahar occurred in 1947 along Kautz Creek, and the next one could happen tomorrow.

A close up view of the Nisqually Icefall, with a rockfall caught in progress (the fuzzy area to the right of the icefall)

Mt Rainier was formed by alternating layers of lava and ash, which can be seen as layers of rock of different colors and textures. It is heavily eroded by glaciers, and geologists have found evidence that during the past 10,000 years there have been at least 60 lahars. Mt Rainier is constantly venting hot, sulfur-rich volcanic gases through fumaroles beneath its glaciers and snowfields. The sulfur gases dissolve into the groundwater produced by melting ice and snow and create sulfuric acid, which then attacks the hard rock and transforms it into clay minerals that are weak and water saturated. Eventually an entire section of the mountain collapses under its own weight, and a lahar is born. The last major lahar occurred only 500 years ago and buried the Puyallup River Valley.

Mt Rainier and Reflection Lakes

There are several picturesque lakes near Mt Rainier. The most accessible are Reflection Lakes, on the south east side of the mountain along Stevens Canyon Road. You can park on the side of the road and see a perfect reflection of Mt Rainier in the lake without even getting out of you car. Another easily accessible viewpoint is Tipsoo Lake, located along Highway 410 near Chinook Pass.

Wildflowers along the Silver Forest Trail in the Sunrise area

The wildflower season on Mt Rainier is short but spectacular. July through August is normally the best time to see wildflowers, but this varies year to year depending on the weather. The glowing red and orange feathery-looking flowers that you can see are Indian Paintbrush (Castilleja miniata), the blue and purple flowers are Broadleaf Lupine (Lupinus latifolius) and the ones that look like little balls of fur are Pasqueflowers (Anemone occidentalis) in their seed pod stage. The sub-alpine meadows around Mt Rainier have been ranked as the best spot in the US for viewing wildflowers, and one of the 50 best spots in the world according to experts.

Indian Paintbrush and Pasqueflowers along the Sunrise Rim Trail in the Sunrise area

Hikers at the summit of Second Burroughs Mountain, elevation 7,402 feet

Mt Rainier is a land of extremes. If you find your senses overwhelmed by the endless meadows filled with vibrant wildflowers, you can hike up one of the many trails that will take you above the tree line and experience the exact opposite environment: nothing but rocks, snow and ice. Mt Rainier has 260 miles of maintained trails, and one of the most popular for an alpine experience is the trail up Burroughs Mountain, an ancient lava flow on the northeast side of Mt Rainier. The trail reaches a height of 7,828 feet, and provides a close-up in-your-face view of the massive glacier carved mountain. It can be a humbling experience to look directly at a thing that weighs over 5 trillion times more than you do (if you weigh 150 pounds).

View from the Skyline Trail, with Mt St Helens venting steam visible on the horizon and the Nisqually River below

Stunning views of Mt Rainier and its glaciers are not all that await you from the higher elevation trails. All you have to do is turn around and look down. From the Skyline Trail near Panorama Point at 7,000 feet you can look down 4,000 feet to the Nisqually River Valley below.

Looking down on the clouds from the Paradise area

First light of the day on Mt Rainier seen from the Sourdough Ridge Trail

My personal favorite spot in the whole world to watch the sunrise is from the Sourdough Ridge Trail near the Sunrise Visitor Center on the northeast side of the mountain. When the sun pops up over the mountains to the east, only the very summit of the mountain lights up. Since the snow and ice is white, it takes on the orange and red hues of the morning sunlight. As the sun rises up over the horizon, the line marking boundary between light and shadow creeps down the mountain. If you look real close, you can actually see it move. As the sunlight brightens, the colors gradually change to yellow and by the time the sunlight hits the valley below, it has become daylight white and a new day has begun.

Edith Creek seen in early autumn from the Skyline Trail

A large well fed Marmot

One of the most prevalent critters you can see at Mt Rainier are marmots, which are related to squirrels and prairie dogs. Marmots make a distinctive whistling sound when alarmed and use this to communicate with each other. When not alarmed, they can usually be seen either basking in the sunlight or eating, and seem to be as curious about you as you are about them. There are 14 species of marmots in the world, and the ones that live around Mt Rainier are Hoary Marmots. They spend most of the year hibernating in burrows and emerge when the snow melts. Big males can weigh over 20 pounds.

Mt Rainier as seen from Crystal Mountain

For anyone that yearns for a mountain top vista of Mt Rainier but who does not want to climb 3,000 vertical feet, there is an answer. Crystal Mountain Ski resort operates the Mt Rainier Gondola year round that runs from the ski lodge up to the summit of Crystal Mountain, 7,002 feet high. There is a restaurant at the top, which has the distinction of being the highest elevation restaurant in Washington State. The gondolas are fully enclosed and each one holds eight people. The ride to the top takes ten minutes and is very steep in some places. Once at the top, you can enjoy stunning views in all directions.

The trail through the Grove of the Patriarchs, an old growth forest on the south east side of Mt Rainier

There is much more to Mt Rainier National Park than rocks, glaciers and alpine meadows. There is an old growth rain forest in the Ohanapecosh River Valley known as the Grove of the Patriarchs. It is home to several ancient western hemlock, Douglas fir and western red cedar trees that have been growing there for over 1,000 years and are now up to 300 feet tall. There is a network of boardwalks as well as trails that provide easy access to this magnificent forest.

Mt Rainier as seen from the Pinnacle Peak Trail

Of all the seven wonders of Washington State, Mt Rainier has by far the greatest amount of user participation in the form of volunteers. In 2014, for example, there were 1,693 volunteers who contributed over 57,000 hours of service. Projects range from simple one day tasks such as minor trail maintenance to long term projects that can last for months or even years. Opportunities are available in conservation, native plant propagation, wildlife biology, campground hosting, tour guides, natural resource planning and construction.

Mt Rainier

Paradise Valley ablaze with the autumn colors, as seen from the Skyline Trail

Mt Rainier reflected in Bench Lake

While Reflection Lakes (see page 13) are by far the most popular and easily accessible location for getting a photograph of Mt Rainier reflected in a lake, I think an even better spot is the much lesser known Bench Lake. This lake is more protected from the wind so its surface can be as smooth as glass, and the reflection of Mt Rainier is almost like looking in a giant mirror. There is a modest one hour hike to get here. The trail is 2.5 miles round trip with an elevation gain of 700 feet.

Christine Falls, along the road to the Paradise area

There are at least 18 named waterfalls in Mt Rainier National Park, and many more that are smaller and unnamed. Three of them, Comet Falls, Sluiskin Falls, and Spray Falls are over 300 feet high. The highest waterfall is three-tiered Fairy Falls, over 600 feet high. However, there are no trails leading to Fairy Falls because of its remote location, so it is rarely seen by visitors to the park. The most accessible waterfall is Christine Falls, which is viewable via a short path that leads off the road to the Paradise area. All the waterfalls are best viewed in early summer during the snowmelt and in the autumn when the seasonal rains begin.

Huckleberry bushes create an explosion of color every autumn

The intensity of the fall colors on Mt Rainier varies from year to year due primarily to differing weather conditions. A wet growing season followed by a dry autumn that has cool nights without frost, mixed with sunny days, promote the formation of anthocyanins in the leaves of huckleberry bushes. Anthocyanins are the red pigments that give the leaves their vibrant intense colors, and are manufactured by sugars present in the leaves. Freezing conditions cause the formation of anthocyanins to stop, and from that point the leaves begin to turn brown and eventually fall off.

First snowfall of the season at Reflection Lakes

The yellow and orange colors seen in fall foliage are produced by a very different process, compared to the formation of red colors by anthocyanins. Yellow colors are produced by pigments called xanthophylls and orange colors are produced by pigments called carotenoids. Unlike anthocyanin pigments, which are created in the fall, xanthophylls and carotenoids are present in leaves throughout their growing cycles, but their colors are masked by green chlorophyll. Sunlight causes chlorophyll to break down so it must be continuously recreated by the plant. When the connection between the leaf and plant becomes blocked as a result of decreasing air temperatures, the production of chlorophyll stops and the yellow and orange fall colors begin to show.

Mt Rainier shrouded by clouds

The weather on Mt Rainier can change very quickly. You can be enjoying warm sunny skies and a little while later find yourself covered with snow. Some days the mountain is completely hidden by dense clouds only to be revealed as the clouds unexpectedly break up and drift away.

Winter play area next to the Paradise Visitor Center

The Paradise area gets an incredible amount of snow, averaging 54 feet of snow each winter, making it one of the snowiest places on earth. In fact, Mt Rainier holds the world record for the most snowfall in one year. From February 19, 1971 to February 18, 1972 it received 102 feet of snow. The road to the Paradise Visitor Center is kept open year round, making the area available for snowshoeing, sledding, cross country skiing, snowboarding, snow camping, or just playing in the snow, as long as the snow is at least 5 feet deep (to protect the vegetation). In the summer months visitors must stay on marked trails, but during winter the ground cover vegetation is buried in so much snow that you can pretty much walk and explore anywhere.

Cross country skiing in the Paradise area

If you want to escape the crowds that can be found at the winter play areas, cross country skiing is available. You can stay on established routes or you can go off into the wilderness and experience complete solitude, peace, and quiet. About 97% of Mt Rainier National Park is considered wilderness.

Mt Rainier with several lenticular clouds

Mt Rainier can create its own weather. It is not unusual for residents of the Seattle and Tacoma areas to see large round clouds hovering above or just to the side of the mountain. These are known as lenticular clouds. Air cools as it rises, and if atmospheric conditions are just right, invisible water vapor in the wind will condense and form clouds as it flows over the mountain, and then revert back to invisible water vapor as it flows down the other side and warms up.

Last light of the day on Mt Rainier as seen from Graham

## Experiencing Mt Rainier

**Mt Rainier National Park Entrance Cost:** $15 for a seven day vehicle pass, $30 for a one year vehicle pass

**Camping Cost:** $12 - $15 at Cougar Rock, Ohanapecosh, White River campground; reservations can be made online at Recreation.gov, Wilderness Camping Permit: $20, Climbing Pass $32 - $45

**Access:** road to Paradise area is open year round, road to Sunrise area, Stevens Canyon Road, Chinook Pass, Cayuse Pass usually open July - September

# Online Resources

**Every Trail - Hiking in Mt Rainier National Park**
everytrail.com/best/hiking-mount-rainier-national-park

**Flowers of Rainier**
flowersofrainier.com

**Mt Rainier Guest Services - Paradise Inn**
mtrainierguestservices.com

**Mt Rainier National Park**
nps.gov/mora/index.htm

**Mt Rainier Photographs**
washingtonphotographs.com/Mt-Rainier

**Mt Rainier Visitor Association**
mt-rainier.com

**Mt Rainier Volunteers**
rainiervolunteers.blogspot.com

**OhRanger.com - Mt Rainier National Park**
ohranger.com/mt-rainier

**Pacific Northwest Seismic Network - Mt Rainier**
pnsn.org/volcanoes/mount-rainier

**RMI Expeditions - Mt Rainier Climbing Programs**
rmiguides.com/mt-rainier

**Scenic Washington State - Chinook Pass Scenic Byway**
scenicwa.com/suggesteditineraries_detail.php?tourid=86

**US Dept of Transportation - Chinook Scenic Byway**
fhwa.dot.gov/byways/byways/2226

**USGS Volcanic Hazards Program - Mt Rainier**
volcanoes.usgs.gov/volcanoes/mount_rainier

**Visit Rainier**
visitrainier.com/

**Washington Trails Association - Mt Rainier Hikes**
wta.org/go-hiking/seasonal-hikes/summer-destinations/mount-rainier-hikes

.

# Mt St Helens

Mt St Helens and pumice fields as seen from the Johnston Ridge Observatory

Mt St Helens has the distinction of being the only volcano in the contiguous 48 states to erupt in modern times, qualifying it as the second wonder of Washington. When the north side of the mountain collapsed it created the largest landslide in recorded history. The debris mudflow (or lahar), reached all the way to the Columbia River, 17 miles away, and was 600 feet deep in places. Mt St Helens lost 1,300 feet of elevation and its symmetrical cone was replaced by a crater 2 miles wide. The ash plume reached 15 miles high and ash could be seen on cars as far away as South Dakota (I witnessed this myself). The eruption on May 18, 1980 destroyed 185 miles of roads, 47 bridges, 250 homes, wiped out hundreds of square miles of forest and killed 57 people.

The lava dome inside the crater as it looks today, 35 years after the eruption

Unlike the volcanic eruptions seen in Hawaii and elsewhere, the 1980 eruption of Mt St Helens did not produce any lava. The process of the eruption was actually four separate events:

**1.** A 5.1 magnitude earthquake one mile deep, which destabilized the entire north side of the mountain;

**2.** A massive landslide and lahar which buried the Toutle River valley in a mixture of ice, water, ash and debris;

**3.** A hydrothermal lateral blast with temperatures as high as 1,200 degrees and a speed of 670 mph, which devastated hundreds of square miles of forest, knocking over millions of trees up to 11 miles away; and

**4.** The actual eruption of hot gas and ash, which lasted for 9 hours.

Two hikers on Boundary Trail

Following the 1980 cataclysmic eruption, 21 much smaller eruptions occurred over the next six years, and during this time period Mt St Helens began rebuilding itself. A lava dome appeared that was formed as hardened lava was extruded from the crater floor. Beginning in 1987 the volcano was relatively quiet and then began another series of small eruptions and dome building from 2004 to 2008. Magma reached the crater and could be seen glowing red through the cracks in the lava dome. Mt St Helens is currently in another quiet phase, but occasionally visitors can still see steam venting from the dome.

The Johnston Ridge Observatory provides an excellent viewing platform

In 1982 the Mt St Helens National Volcanic Monument was established and in 1997 the Johnston Ridge Observatory opened. It was built near the spot where volcanologist David Johnston witnessed the eruption from about five miles away. He was in radio contact with the USGS Vancouver office when Mt St Helens blew, and told them, "Vancouver! Vancouver! This is it!" David was instrumental in getting the area surrounding Mt St Helens closed off to the public prior to the eruption, despite pressure to keep it open, and this undoubtedly saved hundreds of lives. His body was never found. Today visitors have the opportunity to explore the blast zone around Mt St Helens first hand through a network of trails, guided walks and presentations by volunteers.

Meadows filled with Prairie Lupine (Lupinus lepiduson) around Mt St Helens

The story of Mt St Helens is not just about death and destruction. It is also about recovery. Although it will take centuries for the old growth forests to re-establish themselves, naturalists are surprised at how quickly nature has started to reclaim the devastated landscape. Among the first plants to arrive was the Prairie Lupine, which can absorb nitrogen directly from the air instead of the ground. These wildflowers attracted insects and plant eating animals.

A few Pearly Everlasting (Anaphalis margaritacea) breaking through the pumice

Dead plants and insects as well as animal droppings helped to re-establish soil, which then allowed windblown seeds to germinate. Elk, black-tailed deer, mountain goat, black bear, and cougar have all returned to the area. Here scientists have a unique opportunity to observe and learn about ecological succession. For example, it appears that areas in the blast zone left undisturbed after the eruption resulted in greater biodiversity than areas where efforts were made to speed up recovery by clearing out dead trees and planting new ones.

Indian Paintbrush (Castilleja miniata) springing up between pumice rocks

View of Mt St Helens from the theater inside the Johnston Ridge Observatory

If you visit the Johnston Ridge Observatory, be sure to take time to watch the video that shows what the eruption of Mt St Helens would have looked like if you were just a few miles away. It is about 15 minutes long, and after the final scene, the movie screen raises up, the curtains open and you see the mountain right in front of you through the floor to ceiling windows. It is quite impressive.

The Johnston Ridge Observatory, built right into the ridge, is 90 minutes from I-5 and only 5 miles from Mt St Helens

Mt St Helens as seen from a viewpoint along the Spirit Lake Highway

You can hike to the top of Mt St Helens. It is a ten mile round trip with an elevation gain of 4,500 feet and takes anywhere from seven to twelve hours, depending on your physical condition. This is no easy hike, as 3,700 feet of the elevation gain is in the last 3 miles and a lot of that is climbing over lava boulders and rock piles. A permit is required, which can be purchased online at the Mt St Helens Institute's web site. Between April 1 and October 31 only a limited number of people are allowed to climb to the summit each day, so permits for a particular day can run out. Once you arrive at the 8,365 foot high summit, you can look down directly into the crater. Hikers report that there are at least six active steam vents. Access to the crater itself is strictly prohibited for safety reasons.

Mt St Helens and the Toutle River Valley

## Experiencing Mt St Helens

**Mt St Helens National Volcanic Monument Entrance Cost:** none

**Johnston Ridge Observatory Use Fee:** $8

**Mt St Helens Visitor Center (at Silver Lake) Admission:** $5 - $15

**Access:** roads are closed in the winter, Johnston Ridge Observatory is normally open June through October, Mt St Helens Visitor Center is open year round

# Online Resources

**A Riveting View of Mt St Helens**
oregonlive.com/mount-st-helens

**Gifford Pinchot National Forest**
fs.usda.gov/giffordpinchot

**LiveScience.com - Mt St Helens Still Recovering 30 Years Later**
livescience.com/6450-mount-st-helens-recovering-30-years.html

**MtStHelens.com**
mountsthelens.com

**Mt St Helens Institute**
mshinstitute.org

**Mt St Helens National Volcanic Monument**
fs.usda.gov/mountsthelens

**Mt St Helens Visitor Center**
parks.wa.gov/245/Mount-St-Helens-Visitor-Center

**Pacific Northwest Seismic Network - Mt St Helens**
pnsn.org/volcanoes/mount-st-helens

**Scenic Washington State - Mt St Helens Scenic Byway**
scenicwa.com/suggesteditineraries_detail.php?tourid=167

**USGS Volcano Hazards Program - The Legacy of David A Johnston**
volcanoes.usgs.gov/observatories/cvo/david_johnston.html

**USGS Volcano Hazards Program - Mt St Helens**
volcanoes.usgs.gov/volcanoes/st_helens/st_helens_geo_hist_101.html

**Washington Trails Association - Mt St Helens Hikes**
wta.org/go-hiking/seasonal-hikes/summer-destinations/mount-st.-helens-hikes

# The Columbia River Gorge

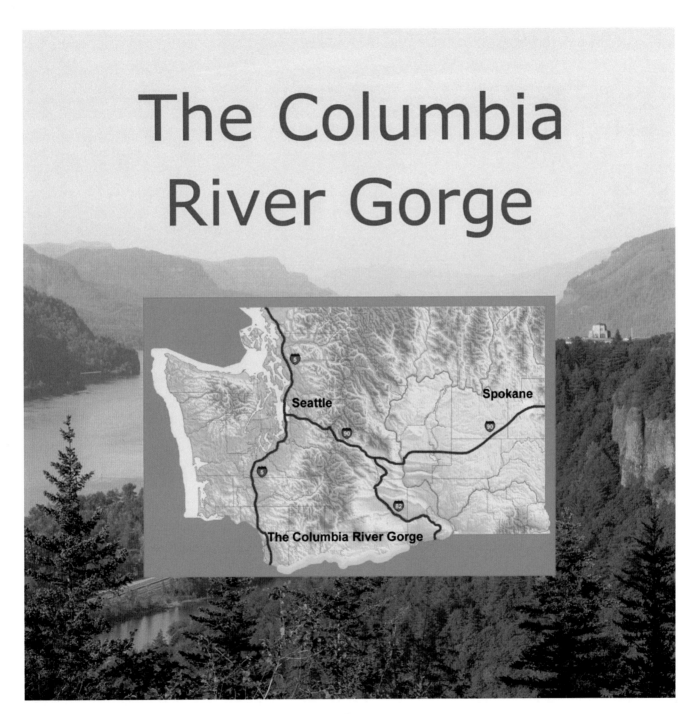

The Columbia River Gorge and the Vista House

It is really amazing to see a river flowing right through a mountain range, and that is exactly what the Columbia River does in the Columbia River Gorge. The Cascade Mountains run from Canada, then south through Washington and into Oregon. The roughly 90 mile long canyon cuts east to west right through the Cascade Mountains, forming the border between Washington and Oregon, and in some places is 4,000 feet deep. How does a river cut through a mountain range? The answer is that the Columbia River was here first. Starting about 17 million years ago, there was a general uplift in the earth's crust that created the Cascade Mountains. This uplift continued for about 15 million years, and it was slow enough so that the Columbia River could keep flowing and eroding away the mountains without becoming blocked.

Looking east from the Rowena Crest viewpoint - note the layered cliffs of columnar basalt visible on the Washington side

Unlike the other six wonders of Washington State, the best place to see this one is actually not in Washington State, but from Oregon. It's the Vista House, which was built atop a bluff 700 feet above the Columbia River in 1918 as a rest stop for travelers on the original Columbia River Highway. It is a good pace to go if you want to be awe struck. Far below, you can see how Interstate 84 follows the Oregon side of the Columbia River Gorge and State Highway 14 follows the Washington side. There are numerous viewpoints along each highway and several parks.

The Columbia River spanned by the Hood River Bridge, with White Salmon on the Washington (left) and Hood River on the Oregon (right)

One of the best locations to get an amazing view of the gorge and to get a serious physical workout at the same time can be found at Beacon Rock State Park. Beacon Rock, named by Lewis and Clark themselves, is the core of an ancient volcano, and is the largest free standing monolith (a single rock) in the northern hemisphere. There is a one mile trail that leads to the 848 foot tall summit. Be advised that much of the trail consists of metal stairways and narrow concrete catwalks that are almost 100 years old that are barely clinging to the sides of vertical rock faces. If you have acrophobia this is not the trail for you! On the other hand, for a quick adrenaline rush, go for it!

Columnar basalt cliffs along the Columbia River Gorge - note their size compared to the freight train

In some places the columnar basalt cliffs rise over 1,000 feet above the river. The Columbia River Gorge is the deepest near Stevenson. As you travel east along the Columbia River the cliffs decrease in height and eventually disappear by the time you reach the town of Boardman.

Eastbound Union Pacific freight train

The Columbia River Gorge is an important transportation corridor through the Cascade Mountain Range. In addition to highways on both sides, the Union Pacific Railroad has a main line on the Oregon side and the BNSF Railroad has a main line on the Washington side. The river itself carries a large number of barges, many of them transporting wheat from the Palouse as well as agricultural products from Oregon, Idaho and Montana.

Orchards in the town of Maryhill

In some areas of the Columbia River Gorge, the Missoula Floods have deposited silt, sand and gravel, rather than cut away at the ancient basalt lava flows. (See The Channeled Scablands chapter for an explanation of the Missoula Floods.) In the town of Maryhill for example, there is enough flat land to plant several orchards. Maryhill was founded in 1907 by Sam Hill, and was named after his wife, daughter, and mother-in-law, all of whom were named Mary Hill. Sam Hill also constructed the life-sized replica of England's Stonehenge as a memorial to World War I soldiers, and the Maryhill Museum of Art, which was originally intended to be his residence. Both are worth seeing and are located nearby.

The Washington side of the Columbia River Gorge is home to several vineyards, such as this one near Maryhill

The John Day Dam, seen from the Washington side

There are 14 dams on the Columbia River, with 3 of them located in the Columbia River Gorge. The John Day Dam, a few miles southeast of Goldendale, has the highest lift of all of the navigation locks in the US. Ships and barges are lifted up 110 feet as they travel upstream through the locks, which are 86 feet wide and 675 feet long. The John Day Dam, Bonneville Dam, and The Dalles Dam are operated by the US Army Corps of Engineers, and all three provide public access via parks located near the dams.

Windy Point/Windy Flats wind farm high above the Columbia River

The Columbia River Gorge is naturally windy. The Cascade Mountains can create huge differences in barometric air pressure between the west side near the Pacific Ocean and the dry regions of eastern Washington and Oregon. This causes the air to flow from west to east, funneling through the only gap in the Cascade Mountains, the Columbia River Gorge. This creates consistently windy conditions. The highlands on both sides of the gorge are now the location of several large wind farms. The wind is also great for windsurfing, and the area of the gorge near Hood River is known as the windsurfing capital of the world.

There are numerous tunnels bored through the basalt lava flows for both Highway 14 and the BNSF railroad tracks

View looking west from Goodnoe Station Road

The climate and vegetation along the Columbia River go through a dramatic transformation as you travel from west to east. Near the Bridge of the Gods at the gorge's west end is a temperate rain forest that can get over 110 inches of rain annually. As you travel east, the climate gets drier and drier until it becomes semi-desert near Arlington, receiving less than 10 inches of rain per year. When weather systems from the Pacific Ocean meet the Cascade Mountains, the air rises and cools, and copious amounts of precipitation are released as rain and snow. This leaves little precipitation for the scrublands east of the Cascades, causing a rain shadow. Possibly nowhere else in the world can this rain shadow effect be seen so dramatically.

Mt Hood as seen from Cook Underwood Road a few miles west of White Salmon

## Experiencing the Columbia River Gorge

**Entrance Cost:** none

**State Parks in the gorge:** Beacon Rock, Spring Creek Hatchery, Doug's Beach, Columbia Hills, Maryhill

**State Parks Admission:** Discover Pass is required, $10 for one day, $30 for one year

**Access (fast):** I-84 on the Oregon side, which follows the Columbia River shoreline

**Access (leisurely):** Highway 14 on the Washington side, which has many tunnels and high viewpoints

# Online Resources

**Beacon Rock State Park**
parks.wa.gov/474/Beacon-Rock

**Columbia Gorge Interpretive Center Museum**
columbiagorge.org

**Columbia Hills State Park**
parks.wa.gov/489/Columbia-Hills

**Columbia River Gorge**
columbiarivergorge.info

**Columbia River Gorge National Scenic Area**
fs.usda.gov/crgnsa

**Columbia River Gorge Visitors Association**
crgva.org/

**Historic Columbia River Highway**
columbiariverhighway.com

**HugeFloods.com - The Columbia River Gorge and Beyond**
hugefloods.com/ColumbiaGorge.html

**Portland Women's Forum State Scenic Viewpoint**
oregonstateparks.org/index.cfm?do=parkPage.dsp_parkPage&parkId=119

**Scenic Washington State - Columbia River Gorge Scenic Byway**
scenicwa.com/suggesteditineraries_detail.php?tourid=626

**US Army Corps of Engineers**
nwp.usace.army.mil/Locations/ColumbiaRiver.aspx

**Vista House - Crown Point**
oregonstateparks.org/index.cfm?do=parkPage.dsp_parkPage&parkId=108

**Washington Trails Association - Hiking the Columbia Gorge**
wta.org/go-hiking/seasonal-hikes/spring-destinations/hiking-the-columbia-gorge

**Windy Point/Windy Flats Wind Farm**
cannonpowergroup.com/wind/projects/wp-wf

# The Palouse

Palouse wheat fields in the spring as seen looking south from Steptoe Butte

The Palouse is the most serene and pastoral of the seven wonders of Washington State. It is a region in southeastern Washington characterized by gentle rolling hills covered with wheat fields. The hills were formed over tens of thousands of years from wind blown dust and silt, called "loess", from dry regions to the south west. Seen from the summit of 3,612 foot high Steptoe Butte, they look like giant sand dunes because they were formed in much the same way. In the spring they are lush shades of green when the wheat and barley are young, and in the summer they are dry shades of brown when the crops are ready for harvest. The Palouse hills are not only a landscape unique in the world, but they are beautiful to behold, making them my favorite of the seven wonders of Washington State.

Different shades of brown represent different crops, land that is fallow or uncultivated, as seen from Steptoe Butte in August

The fact that the Palouse hills exist at all is somewhat of a miracle. During the last several ice ages, glaciers advancing south from Canada ground up the bedrock as they passed over it, creating a fine rock dust known as glacier flour. The glacial flour washed out from the glaciers and accumulated in Glacial Lake Missoula (see The Channeled Scablands chapter). The Missoula Floods washed over eastern Washington and created several huge but temporary lakes. These lakes eventually drained and left behind monumental quantities of silt. Prevailing winds from the southwest blew in the silt and dust to where it settled out into hills of loess that look like giant sand dunes.

Palouse wheat

What is amazing about the Palouse hills is that the particles of silt are just the right size for these hills of loess to form and hold rainwater: small enough to become airborne yet heavy enough to settle out when the wind slows down. The soil formed from loess just happens to have the perfect soil pore for holding the region's scant rainwater. Bigger particles would let rainwater drain through; smaller particles would make clay. Originally the Palouse was mostly grassland used for cattle grazing. It did not receive enough rainfall for traditional farming, and large scale irrigation was not practical. In the 1880's dryland farming techniques were developed that allowed farmers to utilize the unique Palouse soil for farming wheat, barley, garbanzo beans and lentils.

A long abandoned farmhouse, near St John

There are many abandoned farmhouses throughout the Palouse. Farmers typically just work around them, rather than tear them down. Many of them were the homes of their grandparents and great grandparents. Due to the dry climate of the Palouse, abandoned buildings can remain standing for many decades.

A traditional eight-sided barn still in use, near Pullman

Harvesting wheat in the Palouse, near Colfax

The climate of much of the Palouse is classified as continental semi-desert, yet Whitman County produces more wheat than any other county in the US and ranks number 2 in barley. If you drive through the Palouse during the August wheat harvest chances are very good that you will see farmers in their huge self-leveling combines lumbering across the rolling hills. Twice, friendly farmers offered me rides in their combines as I was standing by the side of the road taking photographs of wheat harvesting activities.

Harvesting wheat with a self-leveling combine, near St. John

Productive as the hills of loess were for the farmers, they also posed a serious problem. Some of the hills in the Palouse are steep enough to cause tractors and combines to tip over. Dryland farming requires the land to be plowed along the contours of the hills, not straight up and down the slopes. The solution was created by Raymond Hanson in 1941. During the time period that he was farming in the Palouse when we was only 19 years old, he invented the control mechanism that lead to the development of self-leveling combines. Self-leveling combines.allow the combine's chassis and header (the front part that cuts the wheat) to follow the slope of the hill, while the cab and body remain vertical. Combines such as this one can cut 100 acres of wheat in a single day.

Jessiann, with one of her family's self-leveling combines

"My family has been farming this land for generations. The techniques have changed over time as new information and technology comes along, but one thing has remained constant over the years: we are soil farmers. Our success in wheat farming is directly dependent on the health of our soil. Each generation has the opportunity to take the knowledge and skills of their fathers, and try to make it even better! It is farming with a purpose, it is in our blood, it's what we do! Everything we do is dictated by mother nature. We wait, and watch her moves and subtleties, and when she gives us the signal, we are off and running, mowing, weeding, spraying, fertilizing, seeding all before it is too late. Then we depend on her to give us the rain we so desperately need." - *Jessiann Loomis, fourth generation wheat farmer*

Combines harvesting beans with Steptoe Butte visible in the distance

Wheat ready for harvest, near St John

When the time comes to harvest the wheat, farmers work extremely long hours

Although Washington State as a whole produces less wheat than #1 ranked Kansas, the Palouse wheat farmers have a much higher yield per acre due to their excellent dryland farming techniques. They can harvest up to 100 bushels an acre, twice the national average. Still, it is a lot of hard work. Wheat farmers spend an entire year preparing for a harvest that lasts just a few short weeks. They literally work from dawn to dusk and even into the night to cut the wheat at just the right time.

Grain elevators in the Palouse, with three yellow state owned Grain Train rail cars

During the wheat harvest much of the grain is loaded into grain elevators. It can be stored for long periods or shipped out immediately via truck or rail. The Washington State Dept of Transportation owns 100 hopper railroad cars used for transporting wheat and barley, known as the Grain Train. This program began in 1990 as a way of providing an economical method for farmers to transport their grain to deep water ports in Seattle, Tacoma, Vancouver and Portland. The trains are operated by Union Pacific, BNSF, and several eastern Washington short line railroads. Washington State is one of the few states in the US that owns a short line railroad, the Palouse River & Coulee City Rail System. It was created primarily to serve the agriculture industry in eastern Washington and has been very successful.

Palouse canola fields

Every spring, a few special areas of the Palouse come alive with zillions of tiny yellow canola flowers. Seeds in the pods are used to make canola oil. Canola is slowly growing in popularity with Palouse farmers. Twenty years ago they would typically get 100 pounds an acre of yield for spring canola. After years of research and development, farmers can now get up to 2,000 pounds an acre for spring canola and 4,000 pounds an acre for winter canola. In addition to using canola oil for cooking, experiments are now being conducted in using canola oil as an aviation bio-fuel.

In the Palouse, there is beauty even in the dirt

The Palouse is home to the Palouse Scenic Byway. Washington State was one of the first states to develop a system of official scenic highways. They are intended to highlight our state's scenic, cultural and historic landscapes. There are currently sixteen state scenic byways in Washington, in addition to the six national scenic byways. The Palouse Scenic Byway includes US Highway 195 from Rosalia to Uniontown, state highway 26 from Washtucna to Palouse, and state highway 27 from Pullman to Rockford. However, for a more rugged experience, you might venture out on to one of the hundreds of gravel and dirt roads that crisscross the Palouse farmland. Make sure you have a GPS because many of them are not marked.

Traditional red barn near Uniontown

Wheat in the spring looks almost like grass until you look at it closely

The name "Palouse" is believed to have originated with French fur traders who traveled through the area in the early 1800's. The French word *pelouse* means "lawn". At that time the rolling hills were covered with grass, not the wheat we see today. The name Palouse was also given to the Native Americans who inhabited the area, as well as the spotted horses they breed. Eventually, the term "a palouse" horse morphed into "Appaloosa".

Vineyards amongst the wheat fields in the Palouse, near Walla Walla

A relatively recent development in the southern area of the Palouse near Walla Walla is the appearance of vineyards. In 1972 there were exactly six wineries in Washington State. As of 2015 there are over 800. The same climate that is ideal for wheat is also great for growing grapes, with Cabernet Sauvignon being the leading varietal. The area of the Palouse from Colfax south to Waitsburg lies within the boundary of the Columbia Valley AVA, and the area further south is within the Walla Walla Valley AVA. An American Viticultural Area (AVA) is an official US government designation for wine growing regions based on distinctive geographic features, climate, soil, and elevation. The two AVA's within the Palouse have the same latitude as the Bordeaux wine growing region of France.

Probably a former wheat field

Washington state ranks second in the US in wine grape production, following California. AVA's are established based of *terrior*, which is a French word that can be loosely translated as "a sense of place". It was developed by the French as a way of differentiating the various regions in France where the grapes for specific wines are grown. The terrior of the Walla Walla Valley in the Palouse is very unique, and features four different soil types: loess layered over flood sediments below 1,000 feet in elevation, deep layers of loess in the foothills, cobblestone river gravel in the floodplains, and thin layers of loess on top of the basalt bedrock on steep slopes and canyons. Different minerals, soil composition, climate, and topography all affect the taste of the wine produced.

Part of a wind farm near Dayton

The most recent crop to be developed in the Palouse is electricity. Vast wind farms can now be seen around Oakdale and Dayton. The wind turbines typically have blades 160 feet long mounted on towers 260 feet tall. Each one produces 1.8 megawatts of electricity. The 58 wind turbines near Oaksdale, for example, together produce enough electricity to power the entire city of Pullman. Farmers can receive regular income as a result of wind turbines being located on their property, while retaining use of 95% of their farmland.

Mixed crops in the Palouse near Dayton

Wheat fields lit by the setting sun as seen from Steptoe Butte

# Experiencing the Palouse

**Entrance Cost:** none

**State Parks in the Palouse:** Steptoe Butte, Lewis & Clark Trail

**State Parks Admission:** Discover Pass is required, $10 for one day, $30 for one year

**When to Visit:** April - June for green wheat fields, August - September for the wheat harvest; the best time of the day to visit Steptoe Butte is early morning or early evening when the sun is low near the horizon

**Access:** The Palouse Scenic Byway is always open, unmaintained dirt roads may be impassible in the winter

# Online Resources

**Discover Pass**
discoverpass.wa.gov

**Hopkins Ridge Wind Farm**
pse.com/aboutpse/ToursandRecreation/HopkinsRidge/Pages/default.aspx

**Kamiak Butte County Park**
wta.org/go-hiking/hikes/kamiak-butte

**Marengo Wind Farm**
pacificorp.com/es/re/mi.html

**Natural Wonders: Singing the Praises of the Palouse**
maryjanesfarm.org/about/articlesawards/palouse100702.asp

**Palouse Scenic Byway**
palousescenicbyway.org

**Photographing the Palouse in Eastern Washington**
pullmanchamber.com/visit-pullman/things-to-do-in-pullman/photography

**Scenic Washington State - Palouse Scenic Byway**
scenicwa.com/article/palouse-scenic-byway.html

**Steptoe Butte State Park**
parks.wa.gov/592/Steptoe-Butte

**Washington Grain Commission**
wawg.org/wgc

**Walla Walla Wine**
wallawallawine.com

**Walla Walla Valley AVA**
washingtonwine.org/wine-101/regions/walla_walla_valley.php

**Washington Trails Association - Kamiak Butte Hiking Trails**
wta.org/go-hiking/hikes/kamiak-butte

# The Hoh Rain Forest

The Hoh Rain Forest

Seattle

Spokane

Hall of Mosses in the Hoh Rain Forest

Everybody knows about the Amazon, the world's largest *tropical* rain forest. However there are several lesser-known *temperate* rain forests, such as the Hoh Rain Forest on the Olympic Peninsula. Everybody also knows Seattle's reputation for being rainy all the time. Seattle gets around 36 inches of rain a year. By comparison, the Hoh Rain Forest gets as much as 14 *feet* of rain a year. Wow! The prevalent fog and mist contributes the equivalent of another 30 inches of rain, resulting in one of the world's lushest rain forests, hence its designation as one of the wonders of Washington State. The western slopes of the Olympic Mountains are the first area to get hit with the moisture-laden wind and rain storms that come in from the Pacific Ocean. As the air rises along the windward slopes of the mountains it cools and yields precipitation, and lots of it.

Moss, ferns and other plants in the Hall of Mosses

The Hoh Rain Forest is one of four rain forests on the Olympic Peninsula. However, it is the only one that has been awarded the distinction of being a World Heritage Site and a Biosphere Reserve by UNESCO. Its unique ecosystem has remained unchanged for thousands of years and it is now the most carefully preserved rain forest in the northern hemisphere. The most common types of trees that grow in the Hoh Rain Forest are Sitka Spruce and Western Hemlock (Washington's official state tree), which can reach over 300 feet high and seven feet in diameter. Most of them are covered with huge clumps of hanging moss and ferns. Moss is an epiphyte, which is a plant that grows on another plant without harming it (as opposed to a parasite). Epiphytes get their moisture and nutrients from the air, rain, fog, and debris that accumulates around them.

Moss grows everywhere in the Hoh Rain Forest

The best place to start your exploration of the Hoh Rain Forest is at the Hoh Rain Forest Visitor Center. From there you can walk two short nature trails: the Hall of Mosses Trail, 0.8 miles long, and the Spruce Nature Trail, 1.2 miles long. My personal favorite is the Hall of Mosses trail - it's like walking through a living green cathedral. For a hike deeper into the wilderness try the 5 Mile Island hike. It follows the Hoh River, is relatively flat, and is lined with giant 100 year old cedars, spruce, and fir trees. If you go there on a day when there are not a lot of other visitors, you cannot help but notice how quiet it is. The moss is very effective at absorbing sounds.

Hanging moss in the Hall of Mosses

Most of the seven wonders of Washington are best visited on a warm sunny day. Not this one. The best time to visit the Hoh Rain Forest is when it is damp and raining because that is when the moss is the most lush and green. Another reason to visit during the rainy season is that you are more likely to see an *Ariolimax columbianus* (a banana slug), which is the second largest species of land slug in the world. This is their kingdom, and here they can grow up to 10 inches long and weigh a quarter of a pound. The rainy winter and spring seasons are·also the best times to see Roosevelt elk that live in the area since they move to the higher elevations in the summer.

New growth on an old stump

The Hoh Rain Forest is full of nurse logs and stumps. When old trees fall and decay they provide a base for seedlings to take hold and grow into new trees. Sometimes when the nurse log has completely disintegrated, it leaves the new trees several feet up in the air supported by a network of above ground roots. Walking along the trails, the dense canopy of lush green leaves overhead and the thick carpet of moss below can make you feel as if you are in an enchanted forest in a fairy tale. You can easily imagine a forest nymph or an Ewok scurrying out from behind a giant fern to the safety of a hollow nurse log.

Still waters in the Hoh Rain Forest

## Experiencing the Hoh Rain Forest

**Hoh Rain Forest Entrance Cost:** none

**State Parks near the Hoh Rain Forest**: Bogachiel

**State Parks Admission:** Discover Pass is required, $10 for one day, $30 for one year **When to Visit:** The Hoh Rain Forest is open daily April - November, weekends only December - March, camping and hiking is accessible year round

**Access:** Road to the Hoh Rain Forest is open year round

# Online Resources

**Hoh Rain Forest**
visitolympicpeninsula.org/hoh.html

**Hoh River Trust**
hohrivertrust.org

## Inforain
inforain.org

**Olympic National Forest**
fs.usda.gov/main/olympic/home

**Olympic National Park**
nps.gov/olym/index.htm

**National Park Service - Temperate Rain Forests**
nps.gov/olym/learn/nature/temperate-rain-forests.htm

**National Park Service - Visiting the Rain Forest**
nps.gov/olym/planyourvisit/visiting-the-hoh.htm

**Temperate Rain Forests of the Pacific Northwest**
groundtruthtrekking.org/Issues/Forestry/TemperateRainforests.html

**Washington Trails Association - Hoh River Five Mile Island**
wta.org/go-hiking/hikes/hoh-river

# Long Beach

The World's Longest Beach?

Contrary to the proclamation "The World's Longest Beach" emblazoned on the archway over Bolstad street in the town of Long Beach, the beach here is *not* the longest beach in the world. It should be called the "World's Longest Continuous Peninsula Beach" because it is the world's longest beach on a peninsula. It stretches 28 miles along Washington's southwest coast starting close to where the Columbia River meets the Pacific Ocean and it then extends north to the entrance to Gray's Harbor.

28 miles of sand

The reason Long Beach is included as one of the Seven Wonders of Washington is because of the experience you have when you go there. Looking to the north at low tide, the wide flat expanse of sand seems to stretch into infinity. It is a very primordial experience: the only things that exists are you, the sand, the ocean, the sky, and maybe a few distant specks that are humans. You are alone in the solitude but you do not feel lonely.

Lots of wet sand means the tide is going out

During the first part of April, Long Beach hosts the annual Razor Clam Festival. Razor clam enthusiasts claim that Pacific razor clams are the best tasting clams in the world, and Long Beach is one of the best places to dig for them.  A permit is required from the Washington State Dept of Fish & Wildlife and clam digging is allowed only during open season. The most effective way to dig razor clams is to use a plastic or metal "clam tube" or "clam gun", which is three or four inches in diameter about two feet long with a handle on the top. The best digging occurs one to two hours prior to low tide. Razor clams can grow up to six inches long, and are best served pan fried. They are almost always available at restaurants in Long Beach.

Long Beach as seen from Bell's View in Cape Disappointment State Park

To get an eagle's eye view of Long Beach, go to Bell's View in Cape Disappointment State Park. It is a viewing platform constructed at the end of a quarter mile long paved trail along the top of North Head, which is the rocky headland that forms the southern boundary of Long Beach. It seems like you can see forever from up there. You may also see some of the bald eagles that inhabit the area.

Washington State International Kite Festival

Long Beach is the site of the week long Washington State International Kite Festival held annually during the third week of August. Tens of thousands of spectators enjoy the performances of expert kite fliers that come here from around the world. It is one of the largest kite festivals in North America and probably the closest thing you can experience to Kite Heaven.

Kites, kites, and more kites!

Kite flying activities include kite trains, Rokkaku kite battles, sport kites, lighted kites flying at night, freestyle competition and kite flying choreographed to music. Very spectacular are the mass ascensions, where hundreds of kites are launched simultaneously. The biggest kites do not look like traditional kites at all. You can see them as fish, dogs, tigers, crabs, colorful geometric shapes that spin around, and even a few superheroes.

Driving on Long Beach

Many people are attracted to Long Beach because they can drive on it. Long Beach is actually an official Washington State highway with a 25 mph speed limit. A four-wheel drive vehicle is helpful but not required. ***Beach driving tip***: keep to the right and avoid the areas where the sand is completely dry;  drive instead where it is wet or damp. You will get much better traction this way. Getting towed is expensive, and embarrassing, especially if any of the locals are watching you!

A foggy morning at low tide on Long Beach

Millions and millions of little Velella washed up on shore

Every few years Long Beach turns a brilliant blue as millions upon millions of little sea creatures called Velella wash up on shore. They are free floating hydrozoans that normally drift in the open ocean pushed by the wind that catches their tiny sails. Occasionally a prolonged westerly wind will push them up on to the sandy beaches of the US west coast.

Velella, the largest one shown here is about two inches long and is a "lefty"

Although they have tiny tentacles that can sting, Velella are not jellyfish. Each one is actually a colony of hundreds of polyps and symbiotic algae. The polyps serve different purposes, such as feeding, reproduction or protection. The feeding polyps are connected through a network of tiny canals that distribute nourishment throughout the colony. Velella come in two varieties: left handed and right handed. Viewed from above, the small sail either slants to the left or slants to the right on the oval shaped body. This ensures that the same wind will blow the "lefties" and "righties" in different directions, thus spreading them out across the ocean. The flat body of each Velella contains concentric sealed tubes filled with air that keep it afloat.

There is plenty of sand and water for everyone at Long Beach

Long Beach is an amazing place to jog if you yearn for solitude

## Experiencing Long Beach

**Entrance Cost:** none

**State Parks at Long Beach:** Leadbetter Point, Pacific Pines, Cape Disappointment

**State Parks Admission:** Discover Pass is required, $10 for one day, $30 for one year

**When to Visit:** the Washington International Kite Festival is the third week of August

**Access:** The beach is accessible year round, certain portion of the beach may be closed to vehicles from April 15 to Labor Day each year

# Online Resources

**Beach Driving**
funbeach.com/beach-driving

**Cape Disappointment State Park**
parks.wa.gov/486/Cape-Disappointment

**Discover Pass**
discoverpass.wa.gov

**Horseback Adventures**
funbeach.com/horseback-**adventures**

**Leadbetter Point State Parks**
parks.wa.gov/537/Leadbetter-Point

**Long Beach Peninsula**
funbeach.com

**Pacific Pines State Park**
parks.wa.gov/558/Pacific-Pines

**Velella, the By-the-Wind Sailor**
jellywatch.org/velella

**Washington State International Kite Festival**
kitefestival.com/kite-festival

**Willapa National Wildlife Refuge**
fws.gov/refuge/willapa

# The Channeled Scablands

Seattle

Spokane

The Channeled Scablands

Typical landscape of the Channeled Scablands, as seen in the Drumheller Channels National Natural Landmark

The Channeled Scablands are probably the least known of the seven wonders of Washington State, but they have the most fascinating geological story of how they were created. I still meet people today who grew up in the Seattle area that have never heard of them. What are they? Most of eastern Washington State is either farmland or mountains, but then there are large swaths of the landscape where all you can see is barren bedrock, cliffs and strange rock formations. The early settlers in eastern Washington referred to these areas as scablands because they were not suitable for farming. Their origin was a complete mystery.

During the Missoula Floods this part of Moses Coulee was filled to the brim with a raging torrent of floodwaters

The Channeled Scablands extend from the area around Spokane, west to the Columbia River near Vantage and southwest to the Snake River near Pasco. They are known as the "Channeled Scablands" because they are crisscrossed by long channels cut into the bedrock, called coulees. About 150 distinct coulees have been identified; some of them are hundreds of feet deep. The two largest are Moses Coulee, which is 40 miles long, and Grand Coulee, which is 60 miles long.

Columnar basalt cliffs along Moses Coulee

The bedrock that makes up the Columbia Plateau of eastern Washington was formed by lava flows of basalt. This started about 16 million years ago and continued for around six million years. Geologists estimate that there were about 300 individual lava flows, which created the basalt bedrock that is 6,000 feet deep in some areas. These were the largest lava flows on earth, covering 63,000 square miles of eastern Washington, northern Oregon and parts of Idaho. These lava flows did not originate from any volcano. They came out of deep cracks in the Earth's crust in northeastern Oregon. As the basalt lava cooled, it often formed six-sided columns with vertical cracks that separated each column, which is why it's called columnar basalt. These cracks made the basalt bedrock very susceptible to erosion.

The blue arrows show the main routes of the Missoula Floods

During the last ice age 10,000 to 20,000 years ago, part of a glacier blocked the Clark Fork River in northern Idaho that normally flowed into Washington near what is now Spokane. This created an ice dam that caused the river to form a lake in western Montana. This lake eventually grew to cover 3,000 square miles, containing as much water as Lake Erie and Lake Ontario combined. Then the ice dam collapsed. The water from the lake was released and created one of the largest mega floods in the history of the world. This was first theorized by a geologist names J Harlen Bretz in 1923. His theory was very controversial and other geologists thought he was nuts. It was not until the early 1970's that his mega flood theory was finally accepted, with the help of NASA's satellite imagery that clearly revealed the network of channels carved out by the mega floods.

One section of Dry Falls, which was the site of the largest waterfall in the world about 10,000 years ago

Over 500 cubic miles of water swept across the landscape in a wall of water hundreds of feet deep and washed away everything in its path in a matter of days. The water flow of this mega flood was as great as the combined flow of all the rivers in the whole world, *times ten*. Geologists calculated that the Missoula Floods created their own earthquakes as they thundered across the landscape. The most dramatic evidence of the Missoula Floods is Dry Falls. What we can see now is a cliff three and a half miles wide and 400 feet high. At their peak flow the floodwaters were possibly 800 feet deep at the top of the falls, so the volume  of water, icebergs and house-sized boulders crashing over the falls must have been unimaginable.

Looking south into Grand Coulee, which was carved out of the basalt bedrock by the mega floodwaters that poured over Dry Falls

When the topsoil was all washed away the floodwaters scoured thousands of square miles of basalt bedrock and created the coulees we see today. Once Glacial Lake Missoula drained and the flood stopped, the ice dam gradually formed again and the glacial lake was re-created. Eventually, the second ice dam collapsed and another mega flood was unleashed. Geologists believe this happened more than forty times over a period of several thousand years, and only stopped when the last ice age ended. Each mega flood compounded the erosion of the previous one and culminated in the bizarre landforms we now call the Channeled Scablands.

A rather large pothole located in Drumheller Channels, carved out by a kolk in the floodwaters

When the Missoula Floods swept across the Columbia Plateau, many whirlpool-like eddies (or "kolks" as geologists call them) formed. The floodwaters carried with them millions of huge rocks and boulders. When these rocks and boulders were caught in one of these kolks, they created an extremely erosive force which drilled huge round holes into the basalt bedrock. There are hundreds of kolks scattered around the Channeled Scablands.

A formation of columnar basalt in Frenchman Coulee known as The Feathers, is very popular with rock climbers (see them?)

Most of the ancient basalt lava flows that buried eastern Washington millions of years ago formed columns when they cooled and hardened. The explanation why is quite simple. When hot things cool down they tend to shrink. A hot lava flow covering hundreds of square miles can cool, and shrink vertically, no problem, as the basalt will just decrease in height and flatten a little. However, the whole lava flow cannot pull the edges in toward the center and shrink horizontally. Instead, it cracks vertically, normally producing cracks in hexagonal patterns if the cooling is uniform. If the cooling is not uniform, columns with five or seven sides will develop instead. The thickness of the columns, which range from a few inches to several yards, is determined by the rate of cooling; rapid cooling creates thin columns, slow cooling creates thick columns.

Hanford Reach, once the bottom of a lake

Some parts of the Channeled Scablands do not show dramatic signs of erosion. In some areas such as Hanford Reach along the Columbia River, the floodwaters actually *added* to the landscape by depositing massive amounts of silt, sand and gravel where the floodwaters slowed down or formed temporary lakes. During the Missoula Floods, Hanford Reach was at the bottom of 3,000 square mile Lake Lewis where the floodwaters were temporarily backed up due to the Wallula Gap choke point. Today Hanford Reach is the driest spot in all of Washington State. In 2011 it received less than three inches of precipitation. In comparison, the Mojave Desert in California averages around five inches of precipitation per year.

The floodwaters reached as high as the top of the bluff on the right side of Wallula Gap

The Columbia River flows through Wallula Gap near the Washington-Oregon border. Wallula Gap is the only outlet for the entire Columbia Basin and formed a choke point for the floodwaters. At their peak the Missoula Floods had a flow of 200 cubic miles per day. However, Wallula Gap was large enough for only 40 cubic miles of water per day, which caused the floodwaters to back up and create Lake Lewis. If you have difficulty visualizing what 40 cubic miles of water looks like, think of a lake ten miles long, four miles wide, and one mile deep.

Palouse Falls, 198 feet high

Palouse Falls did not create the huge canyon we can see today in Palouse Falls State Park. The amount of water that currently flows in the Palouse River over the falls is much too small to have caused such extensive erosion of the basalt bedrock. The canyon at Palouse Falls was actually created by the Missoula Floods. At this location the floodwaters were probably several hundred feet deep, *at the top of the falls*, so they easily could have filled the canyon to the brim with a raging torrent.

Looking downstream from Palouse Falls

## Experiencing the Channeled Scablands

**Entrance Cost:** none

**State Parks in the Channeled Scablands:** Steamboat Rock, Sun Lakes-Dry Falls, Palouse Falls, Potholes, Sacajawea

**State Parks Admission:** Discover Pass is required, $10 for one day, $30 for one year

**Access:** highways are open year round, unmaintained dirt roads may be impassible during winter

# Online Resources

**The Channeled Scabland: A Retrospective**
www2.ess.ucla.edu/~jewitt/Baker08.pdf

**Coulee Corridor Scenic Byway**
fhwa.dot.gov/byways/byways/54772

**Columbia Basin Wildlife Area**
wdfw.wa.gov/lands/wildlife_areas/columbia_basin

**Columbia Hills State Park**
parks.wa.gov/489/Columbia-Hills

**Columbia National Wildlife Refuge**
fws.gov/refuge/columbia

**Discover Pass**
discoverpass.wa.gov

**Dry Falls Visitor Center**
parks.wa.gov/251/Dry-Falls-Visitor-Center

**Failure of the Lake Missoula Ice Dam**
uwgb.edu/dutchs/VTrips/LkPendOr.HTM

**Glacial Lake Missoula and the Ice Age Floods**
glaciallakemissoula.org

**Hanford Reach National Monument**
fws.gov/refuge/hanford_reach

**Huge Floods**
hugefloods.com

**Ice Age Floods Institute**
iafi.org/index.html

**J Harlen Bretz**
glaciers.us/jhbretz

**Juniper Dunes Wilderness**
blm.gov/or/resources/recreation/site_info.php?siteid=270

**Legacy: J Harlen Bretz**
magazine.uchicago.edu/0912/features/legacy.shtml

**Mystery of the Mega Flood - NOVA web site**
pbs.org/wgbh/nova/megaflood

**Mystery of the Mega Flood - NOVA documentary**
youtube.com/watch?v=5aALx19USeg

**Palouse Falls State Park**
parks.wa.gov/559/Palouse-Falls

**Potholes State Park**
parks.wa.gov/568/Potholes

**The Scablands**
arstechnica.com/science/2014/10/the-scablands-a-scarred-landscape-as-strange-as-fiction

**Scenic Washington State - Coulee Corridor Scenic Byway**
scenicwa.com/suggesteditineraries_detail.php?tourid=612

**Steamboat Rock State Park**
parks.wa.gov/590/Steamboat-Rock

**Sun Lakes-Dry Falls State Park**
parks.wa.gov/298/Sun-Lakes-Dry-Falls

**Washington Trails Association - Juniper Dunes Wilderness**
wta.org/go-hiking/hikes/juniper-dunes-wilderness

**Washington Trails Association - Palouse Falls**
wta.org/go-hiking/hikes/palouse-falls

**Washington Trails Association - Umatilla Rock & Monument Coulee**
wta.org/go-hiking/hikes/umatilla-rock-monument-coulee

The Seven Wonders of Washington State

# About the Author

Howard Frisk is a freelance photographer residing in Puyallup, Washington. As a Washington State native, he grew up exploring the mountains, grasslands and seashores of the Great Pacific Northwest at every opportunity. Now his favorite activity is taking photo road trips around the Evergreen State, always trying to capture the beauty that awaits those who seek it.

Howard's photographs have been on display in exhibitions at Premier Gallery and Gallery Three in Puyallup as well as the Northwest International Exhibition of Photography and Washington State Photographers Exhibition in Puyallup. His photographs will be on display as part of the *Harvest: The Bounty of Washington* photography exhibition at the Washington State Convention Center in Seattle from July through December 2015. The exhibition will travel to the Spokane Convention Center and Three Rivers Convention Center in Kennewick in 2016. His photographs have been published in numerous Seattle and Washington State travel guides.

**Web Sites:**

HowardFriskPhotography.com

WashingtonPhotographs.com

**Visit the companion web site for updates and new information:**

SevenWondersofWashingtonState.com

# Notes

Made in the USA
Middletown, DE
16 January 2021